D1544700

How Fashion Designers Use Math

by John C. Bertoletti

Math Curriculum Consultant: Rhea A. Stewart, M.A.,
Specialist in Mathematics, Science,
and Technology Education

CHELSEA CLUBHOUSE

An Imprint of Chelsea House Publishers

Math in the Real World: How Fashion Designers Use Math

Chelsea Clubhouse
An imprint of Chelsea House Publishers
132 West 31st Street
New York NY 10001

Library of Congress Cataloging-in-Publication Data
Bertoletti, John C.
      How fashion designers use math / by John C. Bertoletti; math curriculum consultant,
      Rhea A. Stewart.
            p. cm. — (Math in the real world)
      Includes index.
      ISBN 978-1-60413-606-7
      1. Fashion design—Mathematics—Juvenile literature. 2. Mathematics—Juvenile literature. I. Title.
   TT507.B46 2010
   746.9'20151—dc22   2009022683

Chelsea Clubhouse books are available at special discounts when purchased in bulk quantities for businesses, associations, institutions, or sales promotions. Please call our Special Sales Department in New York at (212) 967-8800 or (800) 322-8755.

You can find Chelsea Clubhouse on the World Wide Web at http://www.chelseahouse.com

Developed for Chelsea House by RJF Publishing LLC (www.RJFpublishing.com)
Text and cover design by Tammy West/Westgraphix LLC
Illustrations by Spectrum Creative Inc.
Photo research by Edward A. Thomas
Index by Nila Glikin

Photo Credits: 4: Dan Dalton/Digital Vision/Photolibrary; 6: Maria Teijeiro/Digital Vision/Photolibrary; 8: Photos India/Photolibrary; 14, 18, 19: Radius Images/Photolibrary; 16: Manchan/Digital Vision/Photolibrary; 20, 21: AP/Wide World Photos; 22: LUCAS JACKSON/Reuters/Landov; 24: top: Spike Mafford/Uppercut Images RF/Photolibrary; bottom: © PhotoStock-Israel/Alamy; 26: © Chris Hammond Photography/Alamy.

Printed and bound in the United States of America

Bang RJF 10 9 8 7 6 5 4 3 2 1

This book is printed on acid-free paper.

All links and Web addresses were checked and verified to be correct at the time of publication. Because of the dynamic nature of the Web, some addresses and links may have changed since publication and may no longer be valid.

Table of Contents

Answers and helpful hints for the You Do the Math
activities are in the Answer Key.

Words that are defined in the Glossary are
in **bold** type the first time they appear in the text.

They Make It, You Wear It

A shopper decides if she likes the look of a dress that a fashion designer created.

Do you like colorful shirts? Interesting shoes? If so, you can thank **fashion designers**. Fashion designers are the people who design and create clothes. They decide how new styles of clothes will look.

Fashion designers create many kinds of clothing. They design pants, shirts, and dresses. They design hats and scarves. They even design purses. Most of the clothes they design are sold in stores.

Sewing and Selling

Fashion designers use a lot of math. They use addition and subtraction to find out if they will make a **profit** on the clothes they make. The profit on a piece of clothing is the amount of money earned from selling it less all the costs of making it. For example, let's say a designer makes a dress. She buys the **fabric** for $50.00.

The zipper costs her $5.00. She buys the thread for $3.00. She pays someone who works for her $30.00 to sew the dress. The designer uses addition to find out how much it cost her to make the dress:

$$\$50.00 + \$5.00 + \$3.00 + 30.00 = \$88.00$$

The dress cost the designer $88.00 to make. Now suppose she sells the dress for $120.00. She uses subtraction to calculate her profit. She subtracts her costs from the amount she received:

$$\$120.00 - \$88.00 = \$32.00$$

So, the designer made a profit of $32.00 on the dress.

You Do the Math

Will He Make Money?

A fashion designer makes a man's suit. The table below shows the costs of the materials the designer used to make the suit. The designer also paid someone who works for him $40.00 to sew the suit. The designer sells the suit for $260.00. Did the designer make a profit by selling the suit at that price?

Materials for a Man's Suit	
Item	Cost
Fabric	$128.00
Buttons	$16.00
Zipper	$6.00
Silk lining	$40.00
Thread	$8.00

Coming Up with Ideas

To make new clothing, fashion designers must first decide how the clothes will look. Most designers want their designs to look good to people. That way, people will buy their clothes.

Some designers use their creativity to make their clothes look different from other clothes that are being sold. For example, a designer may create a new type of jeans. The jeans are bright yellow. They are not dark blue like many jeans. Now the designer has created something different. Shoppers who are looking for something different might like the yellow jeans better than blue ones.

Other designers want to make their clothing look similar to styles that are already popular. They think that is the best way to make sure people will buy their clothes. They

A designer may try to create new styles that look very different from other clothing being sold.

try to figure out what trends are popular each season.

Patterns Are Popular

A designer sees that women's shirts made from fabrics with **patterns** on them are popular this season. A pattern can be a repeating set of objects. The designer has looked at many shirts in magazines and on TV shows. She has seen patterns on many of them. She decides to design her new shirts using fabric with patterns, too.

Complete the Pattern

The designer decides that one of her new shirts will have a pattern on the front that has rows of stars. She makes a series of five drawings to create her pattern. The fifth one will have the complete pattern that will be on the shirt. Look at the first four drawings shown here. Can you make the fifth drawing to show the finished pattern for the shirt?

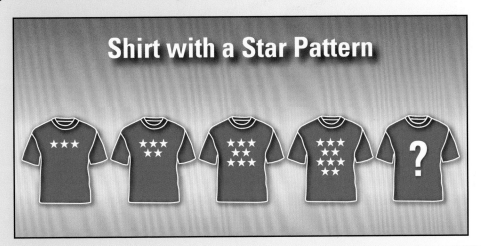

Shirt with a Star Pattern

Sketching the Ideas

Many times, when a designer gets an idea for a piece of clothing, he makes a **sketch** to show what he thinks his new creation should look like. A sketch is a simple drawing. Often, it is not very detailed. The sketch shows the basic idea of how something should look.

A sketch can be drawn by hand. It can also be made on a computer. When designers sketch their clothing ideas, they often use geometry. They draw basic shapes. They draw different kinds of lines. They draw angles.

Many designers use computers to sketch their ideas for new clothing styles.

Clothing and Geometry

Sketches may use circles or triangles. Some may use rectangles. For example, a designer may sketch a boy's jacket. He may use two rectangles to stand in for the sleeves and one for the main body of the jacket. There may be a hood shaped like a triangle. The designer can also use geometry in the design of the jacket. Maybe it will have square pockets on the front.

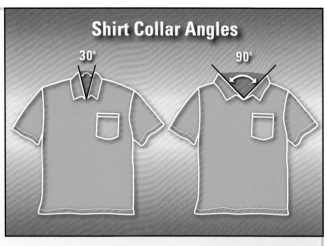

Shirt Collar Angles

30°   90°

Designers also use angles. Suppose a designer creates a shirt. The shirt has a V–shaped collar. The designer must decide how large an angle to use for the collar opening. A small angle will make the collar opening narrower. A 30-degree (30°) angle, for example, will make a narrow collar opening. A larger angle will make the collar opening wider. If the designer uses a 90° angle, the collar opening will be three times as wide as with a 30° angle.

A designer sketching a shirt must decide what size angle to use for the collar opening.

Designers use lines when they sketch. Let's say a designer is sketching a man's suit. The designer wants stripes on the suit. So he draws **parallel lines**. Parallel lines do not intersect, or cross, each other and are always the same distance apart. If the designer wants a checkerboard pattern on the suit, he draws **perpendicular lines**. Perpendicular lines intersect each other to form 90° angles. A 90° angle is also called a **right angle**.

You Do the Math

Design Your Own!

Design a piece of clothing using basic shapes. First, cut out paper circles, squares, and other shapes. Then, use the shapes you cut out to make your clothing design.

Symmetry, Congruence, and Beauty

L ook at the sketch on this page for a woman's shirt. The front of the shirt has buttons going down the middle. On the left side of the buttons, there is a half-circle. You see the same half-circle on the right side of the buttons, except that it has been flipped over. The circle shape on the shirt has **line symmetry**. That means that one-half of the shape is the mirror image of the other half.

Fashion designers often create clothes that have line symmetry. That's because many people think that clothes with line symmetry look good. Many designers give dresses line symmetry. Suppose you drew a line down the center of a dress with line symmetry. The left side of the dress would look like the right side of the dress flipped over.

Using Congruent Shapes

Designers also use **congruent figures** in some of their designs. Congruent figures have the exact same shape

Shirt with Line Symmetry

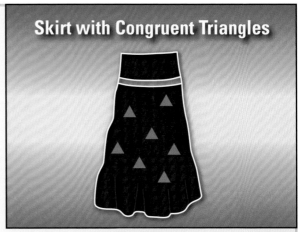

and size. A circle and a square are not congruent. They do not have the same shape. A large square and a small square are not congruent. They do not have the same size. If two figures are congruent, when you place one over the other, the first one exactly covers the second.

Congruent figures can make clothing interesting. Look at the skirt shown above. It has small triangles on it. The designer made sure that all the triangles have the same size and shape. That makes the skirt pleasing to the eye.

You Do the Math

Line Symmetry

Look at the two triangles A and B. Which one of them has line symmetry, and which one does not?

A

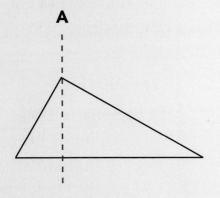

B

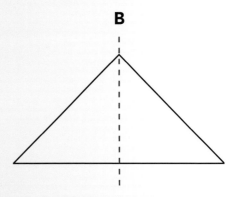

Choosing the Fabric

A fashion designer has her idea for a design. She has made her sketch. Now, she must choose her fabric—the cloth from which the clothing will be made.

There are different kinds of materials that can be used to make fabric. For example, fabric can be made from cotton, silk, or wool. Fabric made from each material will have its own look and feel. The designer must choose which one to use. The designer also chooses what color the fabric will be and whether it will have a pattern. Many designers use fabrics that have a type of pattern called a **tessellation**. Tessellations are fun to look at. They make clothes look interesting.

Tessellations

A tessellation is a pattern made from figures that are all congruent. The

Slide Tessellation

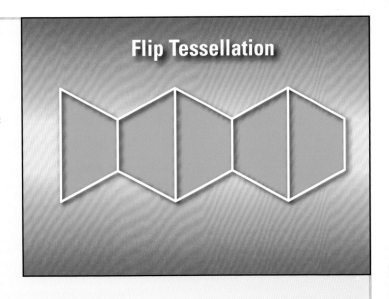

Flip Tessellation

figures in a tessellation repeat. All of the figures fit together like a puzzle. There are no gaps between the figures. The figures do not overlap. Many mosaics are examples of tessellations because they are made up of tiles that are all the same size and all the same shape.

There are different ways to make a tessellation. One way is called a slide. Study the tessellation on page 12. It is made from one figure that has four sides. Each figure in the farthest left row has been slid down and to the right. It is always the same four-sided figure that repeats. It appears many times, and there are no gaps between the figures.

Designers also use flips to make tessellations. In these patterns, the figure is flipped over again and again. The picture above is an example of a flip tessellation.

You Do the Math

Make Your Own Tessellation

Now you try it. Cut out a set of congruent triangles from construction paper or use triangle blocks to make your own tessellation.

Making the Prototype

You know that designers think of an idea, make a sketch, and choose their fabric. Next, they make a **prototype**.

A prototype is a sample of a design. It looks like the sketch, but it is made of fabric. This helps the designer see what the piece of clothing might really look like when it is completed. The designer may use the prototype to work on his design some more.

By the Yard

Designers use math to make prototypes. The first thing they do is to determine how much fabric they'll need to buy. Fabric is often sold by the yard. This means that, often, you must buy a piece of fabric that is some whole number of yards long. If you buy 1 yard

A fashion designer works on a prototype of a dress design.

of fabric, for example, you are buying a piece that is 1 yard long. Since there are 3 feet in 1 yard, you can also say that 1 yard of fabric is 3 feet long.

Most pieces of fabric are 4 feet wide. So a piece of fabric 3 feet (1 yard) long has 12 square feet of fabric in it. You can figure this out by multiplying the length by the width, to find a square measurement, like this:

$$3 \text{ feet} \times 4 \text{ feet} = 12 \text{ square feet}$$

Suppose a designer is making a prototype of a coat. He estimates that he'll need about 30 square feet of fabric in order to make the prototype. How many yards of fabric should he buy?

The designer knows that 1 yard of fabric has 12 square feet. Two yards will have 24 square feet. That will not be enough. Three yards will have 36 square feet ($12 + 12 + 12 = 36$, or $12 \times 3 = 36$). So the designer buys 3 yards. He will have 6 square feet left over.

You Do the Math

How Much Should She Buy?

A designer is making a prototype of a wedding gown. She estimates she will need 80 square feet of fabric. Remember that 1 yard of fabric has 12 square feet. How many yards of fabric should she buy to be sure she has enough?

Measure, Measure, Measure

A designer is ready to make her prototype. So she takes out her **measuring tape**. A measuring tape is used to measure length. It is a type of ruler. Most rulers are stiff, but a measuring tape is flexible. It can be useful for measuring things that are not flat. Designers measure a lot. They measure fabric. They measure people. In fact, of all the math skills that designers use, they probably use measurement the most.

How They Measure

Suppose a designer is making a prototype of a skirt. The skirt will be 33 inches long from

This woman is using a measuring tape to measure the collar on a shirt.

top to bottom. The designer decides she needs a piece of fabric 36 inches long. This gives her 1 extra inch of fabric to make the **hem** at the bottom and 2 extra inches to make the **waistband**. The waistband is a piece of fabric that goes around the waist.

The designer places the end of her tape measure at the edge of her fabric. She runs the tape down the fabric. Then she finds the number 36 on the tape. She draws a line on the fabric at 36 inches. This marks where the fabric will be cut.

Designers also measure people. Suppose a designer is making a long-sleeved shirt for a man. She needs to know how long the sleeves should be. So she holds the end of the measuring tape on the top of the man's shoulder. She runs the tape down his arm. Then she stops at his wrist. She reads the number on the tape. It is 22. The man's arm, from shoulder to wrist, is 22 inches long. So the sleeve must be 22 inches long, too.

You Do the Math

Measuring Fabric

A designer is making a prototype of a skirt that will be 42 inches long. She decides that she needs 3 inches extra for the waistband and 2 inches extra for the hem. How long should the piece of fabric be that she cuts for her skirt?

Making It Perfect with Fractions

When you see a beautiful dress or a cool shirt, do you think of fractions? Probably not. But fractions and clothing go hand in hand. Fashion designers use fractions when they make clothes.

Designers often have to add or subtract fractions. Sometimes a prototype looks too long after it is made. So the designer must cut off some fabric. How much fabric? It depends on the measurement. Measurements often include fractions. For example, a prototype of a skirt may be $31\frac{1}{3}$ inches long. The designer decides it will look better if it is $29\frac{2}{3}$ inches long. To take away the right amount of fabric, designers must know how to subtract fractions.

A designer measures the length of a skirt.

That Collar Is Too Wide!

Suppose a fashion designer makes a prototype of a shirt. The shirt's collar will have a thin strip of fabric added around the edge for decoration. After making the collar, the designer sees that the strip looks too wide. He must cut off some fabric from the strip. But how much? The designer can subtract fractions to find out. He looks at his sketch and sees that the strip should be $\frac{3}{8}$ inches wide. He measures the strip. It is $\frac{7}{8}$ inches wide. So the designer must subtract fractions:

A designer changes the length of the sleeves on a coat to get it just right.

$$\frac{7}{8} - \frac{3}{8} = \frac{4}{8}$$

Now he knows he must cut off $\frac{4}{8}$ inches of fabric, which is equal to $\frac{1}{2}$ inch.

You Do the Math

Fixing the Cuffs

A designer makes a pair of pants. There is a cuff at the bottom of each pant leg. Each cuff is $\frac{7}{8}$ inches wide. After looking at the prototype, the designer decides he wants the cuffs to be $\frac{5}{8}$ inches wide. How much fabric must he remove from the cuffs?

The Fashion Show

The prototypes are completed. They look terrific. Now it's time for the **fashion show**! Maybe you have seen parts of a fashion show on television. At these shows, **models** walk down a runway. A runway is a long, narrow platform that extends out into the audience. The models wear new clothing designs. The people in the audience sit in chairs and watch. They look at the interesting new clothes.

Fashion designers have shows to display their new designs. People who own clothing stores often go to the shows. They decide which of the designs to buy. They will sell clothing made according to these designs in their stores.

Runway Math

Planning fashion shows requires math skills. Sometimes a fashion show can be only a certain

A model shows a new dress design as she walks down the runway.

number of hours or minutes long. Designers must determine how many of their designs they can display at the show in that time. Sometimes designers know they want to display a certain number of designs. How long should the show be to allow all the designs to be seen? Designers can use division or multiplication to figure out things like these.

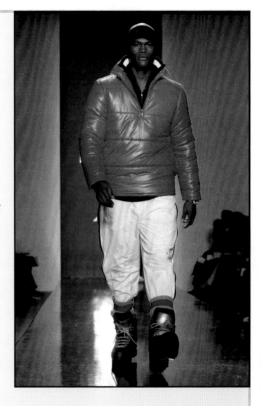

This model shows a new design for a man's jacket.

Suppose a fashion show will be 30 minutes long. Each model will walk on the runway for 2 minutes. She will walk to the front of the runway, stop so that people can look closely at what she is wearing, and walk back again. Then, another model will come out. How many designs can the designer show in 30 minutes? To find out, he divides:

$$\frac{30 \text{ minutes}}{2 \text{ minutes per design}} = 15 \text{ designs}$$

He knows he can show 15 designs.

You Do the Math

The Show Must Go On—But For How Long?

A fashion designer is having a show. She will show 18 different designs. She wants each model to be on the runway for 3 minutes. How long will the fashion show last?

Food and Drinks for the Show

Fashion designers sometimes provide refreshments at their fashion shows. They use their math skills to make sure that they purchase the right amounts.

Suppose a designer is having a show, and 200 people will attend. He will serve bottled water and apples. Then he asks himself, "How much should I buy?" He can use multiplication and division to find out.

Buying the Right Amounts

First, the designer thinks about the bottled water. He wants to have enough so that each of his 200 guests can have 2 bottles:

$$200 \times 2 = 400$$

People attending a fashion show look carefully at the new designs and often make notes about which styles they like best.

So he needs 400 bottles of water. He goes to the store. He sees that a case of water has 20 bottles. How many cases should he buy? He divides to find out:

$$400 \div 20 = 20$$

He buys 20 cases of water.

The designer wants to have enough apples so that each guest can have 1 apple. So he needs 200 apples. The store sells bags of apples. There are 10 apples in each bag. He uses division to decide how many bags to buy:

$$200 \div 10 = 20$$

So he buys 20 bags.

Now the designer is ready. He's sure that his guests will like the water and apples. And he hopes that they'll love his designs!

You Do the Math

Which Case of Juice Should She Buy?

A designer is having a fashion show. She will serve the guests small glasses of juice. Each glass will have 4 ounces of juice. She wants to have a total of 80 glasses. How many ounces of juice does the designer need? Now, look at the table below. Which case of juice should she buy in order to have enough?

Amounts of Juice in a Case		
Type of Juice	Bottles in a Case	Ounces in a Bottle
Ben's Juice	8	32
Tasty Time	6	48
Sweetest	5	64

Making the Clothes

A designer created a jacket. It was modeled at a fashion show. A store owner loved the look of the jacket and ordered 100 jackets for her store. Now the designer must get the jackets made. Her math skills will help her do this.

First, the designer must purchase the materials she needs. She must buy denim fabric for the outside of the jacket. She needs nylon fabric for the jacket's lining. She needs buttons, and she needs thread.

Materials and Multiplication

But how much of each kind of fabric should she buy? How much thread? How many buttons? The designer uses multiplication to find out. Here's how she does it.

Designers use math to know just how much fabric and thread to buy to make the clothing they have designed.

She knows that she needs 4 yards of denim for each jacket, and she knows that she needs to make 100 jackets:

$$4 \times 100 = 400$$

So the designer needs 400 yards of denim.
She needs 3 yard of nylon for the lining of each jacket:

$$3 \times 100 = 300$$

So the designer needs 300 yards of nylon.
She needs 1 spool of thread to sew each jacket:

$$1 \times 100 = 100$$

So the designer needs 100 spools of thread.
Each jacket has 9 buttons:

$$9 \times 100 = 900$$

So the designer needs 900 buttons.
Now the designer can purchase all of the materials.

You Do the Math

How Much Do I Buy?

A store owner ordered 500 pairs of jeans. The table below shows how much of each item the designer must purchase to make 1 pair of jeans. How much of each item has to be purchased to make 500 pairs?

Materials Needed for 1 Pair of Jeans	
Item	**Amount Needed**
Fabric	3 yards
Buttons	4
Zipper	1
Thread	2 spools

The All-Important Tailors

Remember the designer who must make 100 jackets? Well, her materials have arrived. Now the jackets can be sewn. Most designers don't do this work themselves. They hire **tailors** to help them. A tailor is a person who makes or repairs clothing. How much will it cost to hire tailors? The designer uses math to find out.

Designers often hire many people to make their clothing.

Jackets by the Hour

The store owner wants all 100 jackets to be completed in one week. How many people must the designer hire to make them? The designer knows it takes 4 hours to sew one jacket. A regular workday is 8 hours long. So one person can sew 2 jackets per day. There are 5 days in the workweek. So she multiplies the number of days by the number of jackets a person can make in one day:

$$5 \times 2 = 10$$

One person can sew 10 jackets per week. But the designer needs to get 100 jackets made. She divides the total number of jackets she needs by the number of jackets each tailor can make. That tells her how many tailors she will need:

$$100 \div 10 = 10$$

She must hire 10 tailors to make the jackets.

The designer will pay each tailor $15.00 per hour. Each one will work 40 hours. She multiplies the hourly rate by the number of hours each will work:

$$\$15.00 \times 40 = \$600.00$$

So she must pay each person $600.00. There are 10 tailors. Now she can figure the total amount she will have to pay the 10 tailors:

$$\$600.00 \times 10 = \$6,000.00$$

The designer will pay her tailors $6,000.00 to have all 100 jackets made in one week.

You Do the Math

Paying for Sewing

You are a fashion designer. You paid three tailors to sew for you. The table shows the hourly rate paid to each tailor and the number of hours each tailor worked. Which tailor did you pay the most?

Hourly Pay and Hours Worked by Tailors		
Tailor	Hourly Pay	Hours Worked
A	$10.00	10
B	$15.00	8
C	$18.00	6

If You Want to Be a Fashion Designer

How do you become a fashion designer? You need to have talent. You need an education. You must have good math skills. And you have to work hard.

Fashion designers are artistic. They're good at coming up with ideas. And they have ideas about what looks good. To be a designer, you'll need to develop these skills. Study the clothes that people wear. Learn what colors go well together. Take art classes. Learn how to sew. Practice sketching.

Also, learn how to measure accurately. Know how to add and subtract fractions and do other kinds of math. This will help you buy the right amounts of materials. It will also help you keep track of your costs.

Most designers go to college. Some go to a two-year college, and others go to a four-year college. They study fashion design. They learn how to construct clothing. They work with fabrics. They study fashion styles. They learn how to use math to design clothing.

Answer Key

Pages 4–5: They Make It, You Wear It:

Yes, the designer made a profit if he sold the suit for $260.00. If you add up all of the costs, the total cost comes to $238.00 (materials: $128.00 + $16.00 + $6.00 + $40.00 + $8.00 = $198; sewing: $40.00; $198.00 + $40.00 = $238.00). If you subtract $238.00 from $260.00, the difference is $22.00. This is the profit the designer made.

Pages 6–7: Coming Up with Ideas:

Pages 8–9: Sketching the Ideas:

Answers will vary. The sketch should include basic geometric shapes.

Pages 10–11: Symmetry, Congruence, and Beauty:

Triangle B has line symmetry. Triangle A does not.

Pages 12–13: Choosing the Fabric:

Answers will vary. One example is:

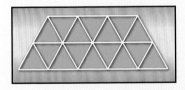

Pages 14–15: Making the Prototype:

She should buy 7 yards. She needs 80 square feet of fabric. If she bought 6 yards, she would not have enough, since 12 x 6 = 72 square feet. But 12 x 7 = 84 square feet, which will give her enough, with 4 square feet left over.

Pages 16–17: Measure, Measure, Measure:

47 inches long (42 + 3 + 2 = 47).

Pages 18–19: Making It Perfect with Fractions:

The designer must remove $\frac{2}{8}$ inches, which is equivalent to $\frac{1}{4}$ inch, from the cuffs ($\frac{7}{8} - \frac{5}{8} = \frac{2}{8} = \frac{1}{4}$).

Pages 20–21: The Fashion Show:

The show will be 54 minutes long (18 x 3 = 54).

Pages 22–23: Food and Drinks for the Show:

The designer needs a total of 320 ounces of juice (80 glasses x 4 ounces per glass = 320 ounces). So she should buy Sweetest juice, since a case has 320 ounces (5 bottles x 64 ounces per bottle = 320 ounces). The other cases will not provide enough (Ben's Juice: 8 bottles x 32 ounces per bottle = 256 ounces, which is less than 320; Tasty Time: 6 bottles x 48 ounces per bottle = 288 ounces, which is also less than 320).

Pages 24–25: Making the Clothes:

The designer must buy 1,500 yards of fabric (3 x 500 = 1,500), 2,000 buttons (4 x 500 = 2,000), 500 zippers (1 x 500 = 500), and 1,000 spools of thread (2 x 500 = 1,000).

Pages 26–27: The All-Important Tailors:

You paid Tailor B the most. Tailor B was paid $15.00 x 8 = $120.00. Tailor A was paid $10.00 x 10 = $100.00. Tailor C was paid $18.00 x 6 = $108.00.

Glossary

congruent figures—Figures that have the exact same shape and size.

fabric—The cloth from which clothes are made.

fashion designers—People who design and create clothing.

fashion show—A show where new clothing designs are displayed.

hem—The bottom of a skirt, dress, pair of pants, or other clothing item. The hem is usually given a smooth finish by folding under the edge of the fabric and sewing it down.

line symmetry—What a figure has if its two halves are mirror images of each other, so that when it is folded in half, the two sides match exactly.

measuring tape—A flexible ruler that allows people to measure things that are not flat.

models—The men and women who walk down a runway wearing new fashion designs to show them to customers.

parallel lines—Lines that never cross. They are always the same distance apart.

pattern—A repeating set of objects or numbers.

perpendicular lines—Lines that cross each other to form 90° angles.

profit—The amount of money a business has left over after it pays all of its expenses.

prototype—A sample or a model of something, such as a clothing design that is made of fabric.

right angle—An angle equal to 90°.

sketch—A simple drawing.

tailor—A person who makes or repairs clothing.

tessellation—A repeating **pattern** made from **congruent figures**. There are no gaps between the figures, and the figures do not overlap one another.

waistband—A piece of fabric on an article of clothing that goes around the waist.

To Learn More

Read these books:

Hantman, Clea. *I Wanna Make My Own Clothes*. New York: Aladdin, 2006.

Kelley, K. C. *A Day with a Fashion Designer*. Mankato, Minn.: Child's World, 2008.

Maze, Stephanie. *I Want to Be a Fashion Designer*. New York: Harcourt Paperbacks, 2000.

Muehlenhardt, Amy Bailey. *Drawing and Learning about Fashion*. Mankato, Minn.: Picture Window Books, 2005.

Stalder, Erika, and Ariel Kreitzman. *Fashion 101: A Crash Course in Clothing*. San Francisco: Orange Avenue Publishing, 2008.

Look up these Web sites:

Fashion Era.com (download fashion sketching tools)
http://www.fashion-era.com/fashion_tutorials.htm

Fashion Game.com (fashion games you can play online)
http://www.fashion-game.com

U.S. Department of Labor (information on fashion design careers)
http://www.bls.gov/oco/ocos291.htm

Key Internet search terms:

fashion, fashion design, sewing

Index

About the Author

John C. Bertoletti is a writer and educator. Though he has a solid understanding of how fashion designers use math, he has no fashion sense himself. In fact, when he goes out, his fashionable wife, Maria, has to assist him in picking his clothes.